Jonathan & Melynda Johnson

Raising Great Kids

In a Not-So-Great World

A Biblical & Practical Approach
to Successful Parenting

DRP

Desert Rain Publishing

Tucson, AZ 85705

This book is dedicated with love and affection to our parents,

Howard and Vimal Johnson
and
Arnie and Bea Ann Ziegler

With words and actions you showed us
how to live, love, give, and serve
Thank you for being incredible spiritual role-models
You have left a lasting legacy

Table of Contents

Introduction

We'll admit right from the beginning: We are not perfect parents. We often make mistakes and respond to our children in ways we later regret. However, we do know who the perfect Father is, and we are passionate about learning how to raise our kids from Him through His Word, the Bible.

Like you, we are striving to raise our kids with excellence, and many of the lessons we've learned about Godly parenting are found right here in this book. We think what we have learned is valuable and hope that this book will offer some real help as you accomplish a most important task: raising great kids!

Raising Great Kids...

This book is not a book based on our opinions of parenting. What you'll find is Biblical wisdom related to child rearing. In fact, as you read this book you will discover that the Bible is a wonderful and trustworthy handbook for raising great kids. Even people who do not believe in God will admit that the Bible holds a wealth of timeless wisdom.

This book will guide you through several key passages and themes that will assist you in raising great kids – kids who will have character, compassion for others, self-control, and the ability to respond to the pressures they face in the real world.

Sometimes we believe that if we have our kids in a good environment, a good school, and a good neighborhood, they will naturally turn out quite good. However, it takes more than an external environment for our children to be raised right. If our children are going to be successful and prosperous, their home life needs to be an environment which promotes wholesome character and strong values.

...in a Not-So-Great World

We love Louis Armstrong's classic, "What a Wonderful World." But let's face it – times have changed. With the threat of terrorist attacks and an increase in the number of violent crimes each year, our world is no longer such a *wonderful world*.

In the 1940s, the top seven school problems were: (1) talking out of turn, (2) chewing gum in class, (3) noise, (4) running in the halls, (5) cutting in line, (6) dress code infractions, and (7) littering. Today, weapons, gangs, and even home-made bombs have made some school halls and playgrounds a war zone[i]. Even elementary and middle school-aged children are aware of the dangers they face as they enter their school.

Even if your kids go to a great school and live in a great neighborhood, children today are influenced by immoral and unwholesome messages that are targeted at young people. Walk through your local mall or check out TV shows aimed at your kids, and you'll see that our children are constantly bombarded by images that do not reflect family values. Kids receive mixed messages about life, morality, and right versus wrong. The emphasis in the media is fundamentally aimed at marketing, not morality.

Raising children today is an extremely tough job because our kids are continually influenced by the world around them through such things as the Internet, movies, MTV, peer pressure, magazines, and video games.

In high school and college we learn a lot about different subjects, such as science, math, and history. We have yet to use an algebraic model to solve a problem, yet we were required to take algebra in high school and college. But no one teaches us how to raise children. No one teaches us the skills and principles to be a good spouse, father, mother, single parent, or step-parent.

Fortunately, God's Word is a timeless resource for living life in the real world, including parenting. My goal is to help you and to guide you through the muddy waters of parenting in the 21st century and give you some practical tools to help you succeed in your role as a parent.

May this book encourage you, inspire you, and impart to you time-tested principles as you seek to raise great kids in this not-so-great world!

Chapter 1

Give Them the Gift of Time

Raising Great Kids

Tim Russert, moderator of NBC News' "Meet the Press," recently interviewed psychologist and talk-show host Dr. Phil McGraw. Russert asked Dr. Phil what he thought was the biggest challenge confronting our nation. Dr. Phil replied, "Right now, I think it's family, frankly."

Explaining the impact of the Internet and media on the lives of our children, Dr. Phil discussed the competition for the parent's voice to resonate in our kids' ears: "We are not the only voice in our children's ear, so we better be the best voice, the clearest voice, the most influential voice in our children's ear."[ii]

Dr. Phil's words reverberate with truth. The Internet and the media play a critical role in shaping the culture, attitude, and beliefs of our children.

"We are not the only voice in our children's ear, so we better be the best voice"
-Dr. Phil

So how do we become the clearest and most influential voice in our children's ear? Foundationally, we must give them our time. There's simply no way to be a central voice in the lives of our children without the investment of quality and quantity time.

A Precious Gift

Time is a valuable gift. It is a gift because you must *give it* if it is to be received. It is a sacrificial gift because you only have a set amount of it. You can make more money. You can make more business deals. You can make more career moves. But you can't make more time.[iii]

No success in the world could ever replace the pain a child feels over the time they've lost with you. Time is simply the one gift that you cannot buy. If we are to raise great kids, we must first and foremost give them our time.

The Bible teaches that parents must prioritize time with their children if they are to raise them right and raise them to follow God. Deuteronomy 6:6-7 (TLB) says: *"You must think constantly about these commandments I am giving you today. You must teach them to your children and talk about them when you are at home or out for a walk; at bedtime and the first thing in the morning."*

> *No success in the world could ever replace the pain a child feels over the time they've lost with you*

We can learn a valuable principle from this Scripture: we must take the time to nurture and guide our children. Take time to walk with them and talk with them about right living; take time at bedtime and in the morning to instill in them Godly living.

The problem, however, is that most families live at breakneck speed today. Both spouses may have to work to make ends meet. Single parents may have an even harder time juggling work, home, and life's demands. Many parents feel too drained to invest quality time with their children because they're utterly exhausted by the time they get home from work.

Some parents will even get home and continue the frantic pace. It seems so many of us have a hard time simply relaxing. There are Internet sites to visit, emails to read, phone calls to return, and projects to complete, not to mention fixing dinner and household chores. When you add soccer, Little League, music lessons, and making sure your kids do their homework, it seems like there is no quality time left to spend nurturing your children.

Busyness is the greatest enemy to time.[iv] Even though we have such great technology today and more time-saving devices than any other time in history, we still don't have enough time.

The truth is, you'll never *find* the time. We will have to make a conscious decision to *make* the time if we're going to nurture and guide our children. What kids need is our focused attention. This is especially a good lesson for men to learn. Some men might say, "I don't understand my wife and kids. I provide everything they need. What more could they want?" What they want is YOU – your attention, your presence, your time.[v]

In America, the average father spends only thirty-seven seconds a day with his children.[vi] We must make the time to express our love to our kids. We don't know how long we will have the opportunity to show them how much we care about them. As Rick Warren writes in *The Purpose-Driven Life*, "Circumstances change. People die. Children grow up. You have no guarantee of tomorrow. If you want to express love, you had better do it now."[vii]

The key to giving our children the gift of our time is to break out of selfishness

Making Time in a Busy Age

People often ask us how we do it. With all that we have going on in our lives, how are we able to invest so much time with our kids? The key to giving our children the gift of our time is to break out of selfishness. For instance, in my (Johnny) self-centered nature, it would be easy for me to say, "I'm so tired I just want to *veg*, watch a ballgame on television, and zone." But I try my best to apply the Bible to my life and to put my wife and children first. Yes, I fall short much of the time. But both of us strive to put the needs of our children ahead of our own needs.

The Apostle Paul said in 1 Corinthians 10:24 (NIV): *"Nobody should seek his own good, but the good of others."* Paul also said, *"Love is...not self-seeking"* (1 Corinthians 13:4-5, NIV). He gave the Philippians clear instructions: *"Don't be selfish; don't live to make a good impression on others. Be humble, thinking of others as better than yourself. Don't just think about your own affairs, but be interested in others, too, and in what they are doing"* (Philippians 2:3-4, TLB).

Applying this Biblical principle of *"seeking the good of others"* will challenge you to make time for your children and to think sacrificially less of yourself. Breaking out of selfishness will help you focus on the needs of your children. And what they need is YOU! We need to have King David's determination. He said in Psalm 101:4 (TLB), *"I will reject all selfishness."*

We encourage you to not allow tiredness, busyness, television, hobbies, overtime, or even church activities rob you of the time you need with your family. They need you!

Time Spent With Your Kids Means Success

There is a whole body of research which suggests that being involved in the life of your kids is the key to successfully parenting. In *Developmental Assets: A Synthesis of the Scientific Research on Adolescent Development,* researchers Peter Scales and Nancy Leffert review more than 800 scientific studies that relate to child rearing.

They report that family support, family communication, and parental involvement are directly related to positive outcomes. "Parental support has been associated with positive outcomes such as lower levels of substance abuse, delinquency, and early sexual intercourse, higher levels of academic performance, and better mental health."[viii]

These researchers also found that parental involvement is associated with higher adolescent self-esteem, self-worth, positive feelings about self, perceived competence, less anxiety and depression, fewer "false" presentations of self to others, and greater interpersonal relationships.[ix]

In short, you have nothing to lose by spending time with your kids, and so much to gain. Invest the time today with your children.

They'll Soon be Gone

Our youngest son, Daniel, has a tendency to be very messy. If there's a glass of juice on the table, he'll spill it! On one rough afternoon, he had spilled his glass, wiped peanut butter down the front of his shirt, dropped his sandwich (which was promptly consumed by our poodle) and was now stepping on the goldfish crackers that he knocked off the counter. I (Melynda) was so frustrated, that without even thinking I blurted out, "Daniel, can't you just grow up!" Daniel looked at me and said in the sweetest voice, "But Mom, I'm only 4!" All too often, we want our kids to be "grown up" right now, when the reality is that sooner than we expect it, they will be.

When you talk to parents of grown children, they'll tell you they do not know where the time went. Your children will be grown and out of the house before you know it, so enjoy them today. Your kids aren't a nuisance; the Bible says, *"Children are a gift from the LORD; they are a reward from him"* (Psalm 127:3, NLT). Enjoy every moment of this gift and reward from your Heavenly Father.

This following story from the late columnist Erma Bombeck has inspired us to not take for granted the time we have with our kids. We hope it inspires you, too. Bombeck tells it like this:

When Mike was 2, he wanted a sandbox, and his father said: "There goes the yard. We'll have kids over here day and night, and they'll throw sand into the flower beds, and cats will make a mess in it, and it'll kill the grass for sure."

And Mike's mother said, "It'll come back."

When Mike was 5, he wanted a jungle gym set with swings that would take his breath away and bars to take him to the summit, and his father said: "Good grief, I've seen those things in back yards, and do you know what they look like? Mud holes in a pasture. Kids digging their gym shoes in the ground. It'll kill the grass."

And Mike's mother said, "It'll come back."

Between breaths, when Daddy was blowing up the plastic swimming pool, he said, "…I hope you know what you're doing. They'll track water everywhere and have a million water fights, and you won't be able to take out the garbage without stepping in mud up to your neck. When we take this down, we'll have the only brown lawn on the block."

"It'll come back," Mike's mother said.

When Mike was 12, he volunteered his yard for a campout. As they hoisted the tents and drove in the spikes, his father stood at the window and observed, "Why don't I just put the grass seed out in cereal bowls for the birds and save myself the trouble of spreading it

12

around? You know for a fact that those tents and all those big feet are going to trample down every single blade of grass, don't you. Don't bother to answer. I know what you're going to say...

"It'll come back."

The basketball hoop on the side of the garage attracted more crowds than the Olympics. And a small patch of lawn that started out with a barren spot the size of a garbage can lid soon drew to encompass the entire side yard.

Just when it looked as if the new seed might take root, the winter came and the sled runners beat it into ridges. Mike's father shook his head and said, "I never asked for much in this life - only a patch of grass."

And his wife smiled and said, "It'll come back."

The lawn this fall was beautiful. It was green and alive and rolled out like a sponge carpet along the drive where gym shoes had trod...along the garage where bicycles used to fall...and around all the flowerbeds where little boys used to dig with iced-tea spoons.

But Mike's father never saw it. He anxiously looked beyond the yard and asked with a catch in his voice..."He'll come back, won't he?"[x]

Give your children the best of your time. Life is short. A great prayer to pray is, *"Teach us to make the most of our time, so that we may grow in wisdom"* (Psalm 90:12, NLT). May we grow wise by giving our family the best use of our time!

There's a piece of prose that says, "A hundred years from now it will not matter what my bank account was or the sort of house I lived in or the kind of car I drove; but the world may be a little different because I was important in the life of a child."[xi]

PRACTICAL CONSIDERATIONS

There are many things you can do to unselfishly give more of your time to your family. We have found that watching movies and television are the biggest time robbers. It might be relaxing to watch your favorite shows on a hectic day, but they won't help you nurture your children and cultivate loving relationships. Here are a couple of things you can immediately do to invest quality time with your kids.

Use the Breakfast Table or Dinner Table in Meaningful Ways

Make sure you devote at least one meal a day with your family. Some find an early breakfast a great time to sit down with the family and spend time together. We recommend you come prepared with a Bible verse that you can share with your kids. This verse might even be a verse that you challenge and encourage everyone to memorize that week. Use the time during breakfast to go over that verse and explain how that verse applies to everyone's life (If you're not sure where to start, we've listed some of our favorite Bible verses in "Resource D: Scripture Verses for Your Family to Memorize").

In our family, we make sure to have dinner together every night. At dinner time, we talk about all the things that went on at school, and we often play a little game. I (Johnny) usually start it. I'll say something like, "My name is Daddy, and the favorite thing I did today was _____." Then we will go around the table and each person will introduce him or herself, and complete the sentence.

Sometimes we even make the game a little more challenging. I'll say something like, "I'm the brother of Luther, and I am

14

looking forward to _____." Then our son Jon-Jon will say, "I'm the brother of Daniel, and I am looking forward to _____." We've played this pattern game for many years, and my kids have never become tired of it. It's a great time for laughter, building relationships, and learning about each others' likes, dislikes, goals, dreams, preferences, etc.

The topic always changes, as there are endless possibilities. All you do is introduce yourself and the topic that you want to initiate. Another example: "My name is Mom, and I'd like to learn how to _____." Then the person sitting next to Mom will say: "My name is _____, and I'd like to learn how to _____."

Teach each child to pray. Model it for them. Your prayer does not have to be elaborate, just heartfelt.

Perhaps you can try this game, or maybe you have a game of your own or an idea for a game. The main thing is to invest time with your children, find out what is important to them, what they are looking forward to, and what is going on in their lives.

Start a Time of Family Devotions

In addition to praying for our children at bedtime, we get together about three times a week for family devotions. This is a time for sharing God's Word with them, talking about their day, and praying together.

There are several things you can do for devotions. You might want to read a Bible verse, tell a Bible story, or discuss a commandment of the Lord. Kids will ask you a ton of questions, and perhaps you will not have all the answers. Sometimes you'll have to say, "That's a good question. I don't know. We'll have to look up the answer."

Always end your family devotions with a time of prayer. Teach each child to pray. Model it for them. Your prayer does not have to be elaborate, just heartfelt. You can say something as simple as, *"Lord, thank you for this wonderful family. I pray your protection over us tonight. Please give us good dreams tonight. Help us to serve you with all of our hearts. In Jesus' name I pray, Amen."*

Or you can ask the children if they have any requests for prayer, and then you can pray for those requests. As you pray for each other, your family will grow closer as you learn to care for each other's needs and concerns.

Mother Theresa once said: "Where does love begin? In our homes. When does it begin? When we pray together. The family that prays together stays together."[xii] Family devotions will be something your children look forward to as you experience quality time with each other.

When I (Johnny) was growing up, my Mom and Dad never missed a night of family devotions. In fact, one of my biggest fears on Friday nights was that my Dad would call family devotions during my favorite television show, the Dukes of Hazard. My Dad liked to read from Matthew, Mark, and Luke, but I was more interested in Bo, Luke, and Daisy!

But today I have fond memories of those times of devotion. Our family prayed for each other, and we were (and still are) extremely close. I can always watch reruns of the Dukes of Hazard, but I can't get those times of devotion back with my folks. However, I can give my children the same experience of family devotions, and you can, too (We give several family devotion suggestions in "Resource C: Devotion Ideas for Great Family Devotions").

As you invest time in family devotions, not only will your family grow closer together, you will also be applying a strong Biblical principle about the way you use your time. Again, Deuteronomy 6:6-7 (TLB) says, *"You must think constantly about these commandments I am giving you today. You must teach them to your children and talk about them when you are at home or out for a walk; at bedtime and the first thing in the morning."*

Take Time to Laugh

Throughout our marriage, we have endeavored to create a home of love and laughter. Our family has fun together. We play together, horse around together, and make each other laugh. Proverbs 17:22 (NIV) says, *"A cheerful heart is good medicine, but a crushed spirit dries up the bones."*

This proverb was written thousands of years ago, and it has taken modern science all these years to figure out that indeed, laugher is good medicine. In a study that was revealed in March of 2005, researchers reported that a daily dose of laughter may be good for the heart because, like exercise, it makes blood vessels work more efficiently.

Dr. Michael Miller of the University of Maryland School of Medicine in Baltimore said, "We don't recommend that you laugh and not exercise, but we do recommend that you try to laugh on a regular basis…15 minutes of laughter on a daily basis is probably good for the vascular system."[xiii]

Not only is laughter healthy; it also helps to cultivate your family's closeness. Laughter takes the edge off of stress, helping to lighten the load and lower our defenses. When I (Johnny) make silly faces and intentionally try to make my kids laugh, it creates an inviting atmosphere in our home. Almost on a daily basis, I'll say to one of my kids: "I'll bet I can make you smile." Every time I say these words, they accept the challenge. They'll look at me with a straight face, trying their hardest not to smile. Sometimes they can't even wipe the grin off their faces in order to play the game with me. If they can actually stop smiling, I'll say: "Okay, don't smile." Sometimes those very words make them laugh; other times I have to pull out the big guns and make crazy faces at them. Sure enough, it doesn't take long before they're grinning ear to ear.

In a *Christian Parenting Today* article, John Trent explains a study that discussed what youth and parents thought would strengthen their family and help family members grow closer together. The number one answer was "spending more time together," and the number two answer was "adding more laughter to our home."[xiv]

Take the time to add joy and laughter to your home. It will strengthen your relationships and foster closeness.

Play With Your Kids

What is it that your kids love to do? Do it with them! I've (Johnny) had my share of tea parties, I know how to dress Barbies®, and I've worn out my mitt playing catch with my boys. As a family, we play Uno®, Monopoly®, and backyard Wiffle® ball, just to name a few of our recreational pursuits.

What is it that your kids love to do? Do it with them!

Playing together gives us a chance to spend quality time with each other and have a great time in the process!

18

Give Them the Gift of Time

In her book, *If Mama Ain't Happy, Ain't Nobody Happy!* Lindsey O'Connor writes, "When families take the time to enjoy one another as they play together, they strengthen their bonds in a way that nothing else can. Parents who play with their children are telling them with their actions, 'I love you. I want to spend time with you. You are important' – messages which children desperately need to hear."[xv]

Take time to play with your children. It will recharge your family and draw you closer and closer together.

We guarantee you that if you will invest time with your kids to learn God's Word together, pray together, and laugh and play together, you will build self-confidence in them as you help them succeed in this world.

A Prayer to Pray: *"Lord, thank you for the gift of my child(ren). I want to give them the best of my time. Please help me to re-evaluate my priorities. Please show me ways that I can ensure that my children get the best of me, not my leftovers. I commit to investing more quality time with my children. In Jesus' name I pray, Amen."*

Questions to Consider:

1. It has been said, "The more time you give to something, the more you reveal its importance and value to you."[xvi] How does what you *say is important* compare with your *actual time commitments*?

19

2. What do you need to eliminate from your schedule to be able to invest more time with your family? How can you reprioritize to spend more time with your family?

3. What is something that might prevent you from starting a time of family devotions? What can you do to overcome this obstacle?

Chapter 2

Rely on the Help of God and Others

.

Parenting. You can't do it yourself. You weren't meant to do it alone. God has given us some wonderful tools to help raise our children, such as the Bible and people.

Use a Proven Manual

The first tool is God's Word, the Bible. The Bible contains a vast wealth of practical wisdom, and we want to encourage you to make God's Word your standard for living. God's Word will help you make right choices and avoid bad choices. The Bible is a light that gives us clear direction for living.

> *The Bible is a light that gives us clear direction for living*

The Bible says, *"Your word is a lamp to my feet and a light for my path"* (Psalm 119:105, NIV). Joshua tells us that obeying God's Word leads to success. He wrote in Joshua 1:8 (NIV), *"Do not let this Book of the Law depart from your mouth; meditate on it day and night, so that you may be careful to do everything written in it. Then you will be prosperous and successful."*

If you want your children to be prosperous and succeed in life, make God's Word an everyday part of *your* life and their life.

In addition to spending time with your kids for devotions, we want to encourage you to set aside a time everyday where you can read God's Word and allow it to speak to you. Your local Christian bookstore will have several resources to help you, including devotional books. Such books will help you apply God's Word to your life.

We've developed a tool called *Spiritual Growth Notebook* that we share with our church family. The notebook is divided into four sections:

- Prayer Requests
- Application of Daily Bible Reading
- Teaching Notes from Sunday
- Hiding God's Word in my Heart – Scripture Memorization

This notebook is designed to help you pray, read your Bible and apply it to your life, take notes from Sunday sermons, and memorize God's Word. In essence, the *Spiritual Growth Notebook* is a journal of your spiritual growth and the lessons God is teaching you (for information about getting a copy of this notebook, visit www.pathwayofhope.net).

There are many such tools you can use to make God's Word an everyday part of your life. Or you simply might want to open your Bible, read, and see what God has in store for you. Proverbs is a great book in the Bible to read that will help you with practical living.

Whatever approach you use, learn what God's Word says because this is our best instructional manual for all areas of our lives: our marriages, our relationships, our money, and our parenting.

A Biblical Foundation for Living

In the New Testament, Timothy is a young man who was given a Biblical foundation for living from his mother, Eunice.

The Apostle Paul mentored Timothy and spoke highly of Timothy. Paul even said, *"I have no one else like Timothy"* (Philippians 2:20, NLT). Timothy became such a trustworthy young man because of his Godly upbringing.

When Paul was encouraging Timothy in 2 Timothy 3:14-15 (NLT), Paul told him to remain faithful to those things that he had been taught from his early days, *"You know they are true, for you know you can trust those who taught you. You have been taught the holy Scriptures from childhood, and they have given you the wisdom to receive the salvation that comes by trusting in Christ Jesus."*

Timothy's mother taught him Biblical living at an early age, and this gave Timothy the wisdom to receive salvation.

Timothy's mom instilled in Timothy a passion for Scripture. It was the manual she used to train her child, and it's the same one we can use to give our children a Biblical foundation for living.

When our children's lives are built on God's Word, they will have a firm foundation to withstand the pressures of life

We once watched a documentary on television about California earthquakes. Because we were living in the San Francisco Bay area at the time, this documentary was of extreme interest to us. We learned a notable fact about the 1989 Loma Prieta earthquake that destroyed the Nimitz freeway in Oakland and took the lives of many people. The Nimitz freeway was a double-decker freeway that partially collapsed. The part that collapsed, causing death and devastation, was built on landfill that was trucked in during the construction of the freeway. The part that stood strong, however, was built on the natural ground; the firm ground that had been in place since the beginning of time gave the concrete structure the foundation it needed to withstand the pressure of the 7.0 quake.

In the same way, when our children's lives are built on God's Word, they will have a firm foundation to withstand the pressures of life. Eunice knew the importance of building her son's life on such a foundation. The Scriptures she used to train Timothy were from the Old Testament, so she would have been keenly aware of Deuteronomy 11:18-21 (NIV). That passage stresses the following about teaching our children God's Word:

> *"Fix these words of mine in your hearts and minds; tie them as symbols on your hands and bind them on your foreheads. Teach them to your children, talking about them when you sit at home and when you walk along the road, when you lie down and when you get up. Write them on the doorframes of your houses and on your gates, so that your days and the days of your children may be many in the land that the LORD swore to give your forefathers, as many as the days that the heavens are above the earth."*

If you want to raise great kids who will be prosperous and successful in all they do, instill in them a passion for God's Word. At the same time, your passion for obeying and applying God's Word will assist you in every area of your life, including parenting.

> *If you want to raise great kids who will be prosperous and successful in all they do, instill in them a passion for God's Word*

Rely on the Help of Others

Sometimes we're tempted to do everything ourselves. But God wants us to rely on others for help. The Bible contains more than 50 "one another" commands. We are to do such things as carry each other's burdens (Galatians 6:2), encourage one another (Hebrews 10:25), and lend a hand to each other (Ecclesiastes 4:10). Peter said, *"God has given each of you some special abilities; be sure to use them to help each other, passing on to others God's many kinds of blessings"* (1 Peter 4:10, TLB).

Don't feel like a failure if you need to ask for help or advice from a friend or family member. Bringing up great kids is not an easy task, and sometimes you will need help and encouragement from people you trust.

Another place to get help raising your children is a church family. We want to encourage you to get into a church that has a huge vision for family and children's ministries. It won't take you long to notice if the church values children. Basically, if your children love going to church – even beg you to go – the church most likely has a vision for helping you raise great kids.

Another place to get help raising your children is a church family

At Pathway of Hope Foursquare Church, the church we pastor, we make our values clear and explicit. We let people know up front that we value such things as excellence, dreaming dreams, teamwork, relationships, and family and children's ministries. In fact, a core part of our ministry is teaching children character and Godly values in a fun and creative environment.

When I (Johnny) was a kid, I didn't like going to church. It was boring. The sermons were boring. The Sunday school class was boring. It was a drag!

My kids look forward to going to church and their friends look forward to going with them. In fact, there have been quite a

27

few Saturday night sleepovers with our kids' friends who want to come to church with us Sunday morning. We've intentionally created an environment at our church where kids can learn about Jesus in a fun and creative atmosphere. If kids feel valued and have a great time, kids will beg their parents to go to church. In fact, we're embarrassed to admit this, but we have even used church as a tool to encourage better behavior from our children (please don't follow our example on this one!).

When we were serving as senior pastors at New Hope Christian Fellowship in Hayward, CA, we had an incredible Wednesday night children's program called "Kidztown." On Wednesdays, we could be sure that our kids' rooms were clean and that they were courteous to each other, because if they behaved poorly, we might say, "Listen. If you don't want to go to church tonight, keep acting the way you're acting." We don't make such threats any more, but the point is our kids did not want to miss church. And to this day, church is the highlight of their week!

You will find that churches with a vision for children and families will help you in the process of raising great kids. The Godly character and principles that you are teaching at home will be reinforced through the ministry of a church which has a passion for teaching and nurturing children.

You can also find great help through support or home fellowship groups. If you are a woman reading this book and have preschoolers, a great

The Godly character and principles that you are teaching at home will be reinforced through the ministry of a church which has a passion for teaching and nurturing children

28

organization is MOPS, or *Mothers of Preschoolers.* Even if your children are older, you can be a mentoring Mom at MOPS, networking and building relationships with other moms. (I [Johnny] thought about starting a dad's group called "DOPS, or *Dad's of Preschoolers,* but I thought our wives would pronounce it "Dopes," so I shelved that idea!).

If you live in the Tucson, AZ, area, please feel free to check out the MOPS group at Pathway of Hope Foursquare Church. Log onto our website, www.pathwayofhope.net, for more information regarding meeting times and locations.

PRACTICAL CONSIDERATIONS

There are many ways you can allow God and others to help you in your parenting journey. Listed below are some suggestions.

Start a Daily Quiet Time

If you are determined to make the Bible your standard of living, we encourage you to establish a daily quiet time. A quiet time is time spent with the Lord for the expressed purpose of building a personal relationship with Him. Pick a consistent time you can meet with the Lord, in a quiet place, if possible. If you're using the *Spiritual Growth Notebook* or another devotional tool, take it with you, along with your Bible and a pen, and journal the lessons God teaches you from His Word.

Help Your Children Memorize Scripture

Pick a Bible verse each week that you and your family can memorize (see "Resource D: Scripture Verses for Your Family to Memorize"). You can go over your Scripture memory verse at breakfast time, dinner time, during your family devotions, or on the way to or from church or school.

Some parents even offer rewards to their children for Scripture memorization, such as a trip to the ice cream parlor after they've memorized three or four new verses. The important thing is to encourage your children to hide God's Word in their hearts and memorize Bible verses. The Bible says in Psalm 119:9-11 (NIV), *"How can a young man keep his way pure? By living according to your word. I seek you with all my heart; do not let me stray from your commands. I have hidden your word in my heart that I might not sin against you."*

God's Word is the best deterrent against ungodly and unwholesome living. As your family learns Bible verses and hides it in their hearts, it will help all of you draw closer to God as you learn to build Godly character.

Find a Church Home if You Don't Have One

If you don't have a church home, visit a church with a strategic emphasis on family and children's ministries. There are many churches that are passionate about instructing children in exciting and creative ways. Learn what the church values and make sure they are committed to nurturing children and youth. The more support you have, the more successful you will be raising great kids.

A Prayer to Pray: *"Lord, help me to raise my kids to walk in the right path. As I'm learning about the Biblical principles of parenting, I ask you to give me a desire to read your Word, apply it to my life, and help my children learn what Your Word says as they apply it to their lives. I also ask that you would put me around other Christian parents, so I can learn from them and grow in my parenting skills. In Jesus' name I pray, Amen.*

Questions to Consider:

1. What steps can I take to read God's Word every day?

2. What two things can I do to ensure my children are learning and applying God's Word to their lives?

3. What things might prevent me from helping my children memorize Scripture with me?

Chapter 3

Establish Character in Them

As parents, many of us are committed to teaching our children good manners and positive behavior. In fact, one of the greatest thrills we get as parents is going to a restaurant with our family and having waitresses or other customers compliment our kids on their good behavior.

Character, however, goes beyond good manners and behavior. Character is the inner qualities and traits that define us as who we are and what we value. We've heard some people define character as who you are when no one is looking. Webster's defines character as "the aggregate of features and traits that form the individual nature of a person or thing." We hope this chapter inspires you to continue to establish the inner qualities and traits that will help your children succeed in life.

What kind of character do you want your children to have?

We want to suggest six character qualities for you to develop and nurture within your children: trustworthiness, respect, responsibility, fairness, caring, and citizenship.[xvii] These are the character qualities taught by CHARACTER COUNTS!, a nonprofit organization that has helped nearly 1000 schools across the country establish character as an education framework. Several studies, in fact, show that building these six character traits improves academic performance, behavior, and attitude.

The Six Pillars of Character:
Trustworthiness
Respect
Responsibility
Fairness
Caring
Citizenship

Even though CHARACTER COUNTS! Is not a Christian organization, the six character qualities are foundational principles of Godly living. Let's look at what the Bible says regarding each of these pillars of character.

Trustworthiness

All throughout the Bible, God uses men and women who are trustworthy and dependable. When Nehemiah selected individuals to be in charge of God's house, the men he selected were chosen *"...because these men were considered trustworthy"* (Nehemiah 13:13, NIV). God used Daniel because of his trustworthiness. Daniel's enemies tried to find fault in him but couldn't. *"The administrators and the satraps tried to find grounds for charges against Daniel in his conduct of government affairs, but they were unable to do so. They could find no corruption in him, because he was trustworthy and neither corrupt nor negligent"* (Daniel 6:4, NIV). When Moses was overburdened by all of his responsibilities, his father-in-law said, *"Select capable men from all the people - men who fear God, trustworthy men who hate dishonest gain"* (Exodus 18:21, NIV).

As we raise our children to be trustworthy, we must instill in them a passion for honesty. It's natural for children to tell lies and be dishonest. Our kids, as cute as they are as infants and toddlers, are born as sinners, and they need to be taught that God desires honesty. Psalm 51:5-6 (NLT) says, *"I was born a sinner - yes, from the moment my mother conceived me. But you desire honesty from the heart, so you can teach me to be wise in my inmost being."*

When children lack honesty, they tend to tell lies, cheat, steal, or be sneaky or deceptive. The first way you will instill character in your children is to clearly confront them when they are dishonest. When you catch your child in a lie or exhibiting dishonesty, allow your child to experience negative consequences proportionate to his or her bad behavior.

This might mean not allowing your child to watch or do certain things. It might mean taking away a privilege, like not letting your child play their Gameboy® or go to a friend's house. Or it may even mean spanking your child (as controversial as this may be). The Bible says in Proverbs 23:13-14 (NLT), *"Don't fail to correct your children. They won't die if you spank them. Physical discipline may well save them from death."* A word of caution: Never, ever, ever, spank your children when you are angry. If you spank your kids when you are mad, you spank them for your benefit and not theirs. When I (Johnny) was a child, my Dad would calmly say, "Johnny, I'm spanking you because I love you." I remember thinking, "Boy, I'm glad he doesn't hate me...I'd be in trouble!"

If you're going to establish honesty in your children, you must model honesty in all that you do

Spanking and other forms of discipline are for the benefit of your children. "The goal of discipline is not to control or break the will. The goal is to build within our children a wise, internal standard that will guide them when they have to make moral choices on their own."[xviii] The correction you give your children will yield lifelong results.

Finally, if you're going to establish honesty in your children, you must model honesty in all that you do. Recently, we were in the shoe section of a department store. We overheard a mother chastising her teenage daughter for her honesty. The daughter was holding a cell phone (the dad must have been on the phone), and the mother said, "I told you to tell him we were in the checkout line getting ready to leave!" Not only did the mother lie; she was teaching her daughter to lie as well.

The Bible says, *"It is a wonderful heritage to have an honest father"* (Proverbs 20:7, TLB). It's a wonderful heritage because when a parent is honest, a child will learn to live upright as well through the example of his or her parent. Your kids will notice when you tell white lies and when you are dishonest. Model honesty in all that you do.

Another aspect of trustworthiness is reliability. We can teach our children to be reliable by teaching them to keep their promises and be dependable. The Bible says, *"It is better to say nothing than to promise something that you don't follow through on"* (Ecclesiastes 5:5, NLT).

If your kids say they are going to do something, hold them to it. Make sure they follow through with what they say they're going to do. In the same way, if you make a promise to your kids, set a good example by doing what you say you're going to do.

The Psalmist cried out, *"Lord! Help! Godly men are fast disappearing. Where in all the world can dependable men be found? Everyone deceives and flatters and lies. There is no sincerity left"* (Psalm 12:1-2, NLT). These words ring true today, also. Dependable people are hard to find. May these dependable people be found in our homes! If we are to raise great kids in this not-so-great world, we must teach them to be reliable by modeling dependability in all we do.

God loves trustworthiness and honors those who display this essential character. The Bible says, *"The trustworthy will get a rich reward"* (Proverbs 28:20, NLT). At the same time, God despises dishonesty. In fact, of the seven things that God absolutely detests (Proverbs 6:16-19, NIV), two deal specifically with lack of trustworthiness: *"a lying tongue"* and *"a false witness who pours out lies."*

God hates dishonesty. The Bible says:

- *"The LORD hates cheating, but he delights in honesty"* (Proverbs 11:1, NLT).
- *"The LORD hates people with twisted hearts, but he delights in those who have integrity"* (Proverbs 11:20, NLT).
- *"The LORD hates those who don't keep their word, but he delights in those who do"* (Proverbs 12:22, NLT).

In order to raise trustworthy children, teach your kids to:

- Tell the truth and nothing but the truth
- Be sincere
- Keep their promises
- Honor their word and commitments
- Be dependable
- Do what they are supposed to do
- Return what they borrow
- Pay their debts
- Not touch what doesn't belong to them
- Be on time[xix]

Respect

Our youngest son, Daniel, plays on a T-ball Little League team (T-ball's namesake comes from the fact that kids hit off of a pole [a *tee*] that is attached to home plate). At one game, a little boy on the opposite team went up to the tee and swung and missed, hitting the tee and knocking the baseball down to the ground. All of his teammates started laughing hysterically. The coach did nothing but put the baseball back onto the tee.

How did that little boy feel? His feelings were devastated. He stood at the tee fighting tears of embarrassment. If our kids are going to demonstrate good character, we must teach them to show consideration of others and to avoid embarrassing others. The Bible says, *"Show respect for everyone"* (1 Peter 2:17, NLT).

"People show respect in many ways. They speak and act kindly, avoid insults, cruel comments and rude language. They are courteous and considerate to family members and treat others fairly."[xx]

If you want your child to learn respect, they must foundationally learn and apply the Golden Rule. Jesus gave us this rule in Luke 6:31 (NIV). Jesus said, *"Do to others as you would have them do to you."*

The principle we must teach our children is clear: Treat others the way you yourself want to be treated. It is easy for a child to make fun of another child or put someone down. But if that child is taught to put himself or herself in the shoes of the other person, it will help them realize that this unkindness hurts.

If you find your child laughing at, making fun of, or putting down someone else, be sure to bring up the Golden Rule. Luke 6:31 is a verse you're going to want to memorize, as it will help you remind your children of the importance of giving respect to others.

If you want to establish respect in your children, here are some practical tips. Teach your kids to:

- Patiently wait their turn
- Be quiet if others are talking
- Treat others the way they want to be treated
- Value and honor all people
- Respect others' property
- Accept those who are different than them
- Use good manners such as "please" and "thank you"
- Avoid insults and ridicule to embarrass or hurt others[xxi]

Responsibility

If we are going to raise kids who turn into responsible adults, they must learn the character trait of responsibility now.

Responsibility is about helping our children meet their obligations. Kids are fairly consistent about shirking their duties, such as chores, keeping their rooms clean, practicing their music lessons, and procrastinating on their homework. There's a great principle we can teach them from Ecclesiastes 8:2 (TLB): *"Don't always be trying to get out of doing your duty, even when it's unpleasant. For the king punishes those who disobey."*

There are unpleasant duties children must perform, but what great preparation for adulthood! All of us need to tend to things we would rather avoid, but good character is knowing and doing your duty and meeting all of your obligations. Not only should we teach our children to meet their obligations; we must teach them to give their best efforts and pursue excellence in all they do.

In the Old Testament, the life of Daniel serves as an inspiration to both of us. He demonstrated excellence at all times. None were found equal to him and his three friends. The Bible says, *"In every matter of wisdom and understanding about which the king questioned them, he found them ten times better than all the magicians and enchanters in his whole kingdom"* (Daniel 1:20, NIV).

Daniel receives promotion after promotion because he gave everything 100 percent. Daniel 6:3 (NKJV) says, *"Then this Daniel distinguished himself above the governors and satraps, because an excellent spirit was in him; and the king gave thought to setting him over the whole realm."*

If your children learn to work and serve with excellence, others will know your kids can be counted on to give their best efforts.

How do you inspire your kids with excellence? The Apostle Paul tells us: *"Whatever you do, work at it with all your heart, as working for the Lord, not for men, since you know that you will receive an inheritance from the Lord as a reward. It is the Lord Christ you are serving"* (Colossians 3:23-24, NIV).

Whether it's playing sports, cleaning their room, or whatever task your kids need to do, they need to realize they are ultimately doing it for God.

David Leeman is a wonderful man at the church we pastored in Hayward, CA, who asked if he could mow the church lawns each week. I (Johnny) said, "David, that would be great! You know that when you do that, you are doing it for God." And I explained Colossians 3:23-24 to him.

On the next Sunday, he said, "Pastor, did you notice the lawns?" I said, "David, the lawns look awesome. Thanks! Great job." Then David said, "Yeah, because I knew I was doing it for God, I did it better than I would have done it if I were doing it for myself!"

That's a spirit of excellence!

There are several practical ways to instill responsibility into your children. Teach them to:

- Acknowledge and meet all of their obligations and duties
- Accept responsibility for the consequences of their choices
- Persevere and not quit
- Work hard and do their best at whatever they do
- Fight against a mediocre spirit that is satisfied with doing only what they have to do
- Not be lazy[xxii]

Fairness

Life is not fair. People are not fair. Only God is fair. Because people are unfair, your children will experience unfairness in sports, in school, with their friends, and when they get jobs.

When I (Johnny) was a freshman in high school, I didn't make the basketball team. There were only a certain number of kids allowed on the team, and many were cut. Two boys who made the team were worse than many of the kids who were cut

One of these boys was the coach's son, and the other boy was the son's best friend.

I learned a valuable lesson: life is not fair. In such an unfair world, instilling the character of fairness is challenging, yet crucial.

It's crucial first of all because God is a fair God. *"God is a judge who is perfectly fair. He is angry with the wicked every day"* (Psalm 7:11, NLT). Being fair is also vital because, just as God is fair, He wants us to be fair. *"The Lord demands fairness in every business deal. He established this principle"* (Proverbs 16:11, TLB).

Our kids know all about fairness. If I (Melynda) take our girls to the store with me, the boys will cry out, "That's not fair!" If I take my boys with me, the girls shout, "That's not fair!" The best solution for me is to take all four kids! Or if I take two kids with me in the evening somewhere, I'll take the other two in the morning. I'm endeavoring to be just and fair in all that I do so I will model fairness to them.

One thing we refuse to do is leave any of our children out of activities. Our youngest son, Daniel, is five. We recently played Uno® as a family. Daniel doesn't fully understand the concept of the game, and the other kids suggested that he could watch a movie while we all played the game. Of course, Daniel was sad. *That's* not fair! We were able to teach the kids about fairness through this incident and how it feels to be left out. Daniel played on my (Melynda) "team," and we all had a great time.

There are several ways you can instill fairness in your children. Teach your children to:

- Treat people equally
- Not leave out friends and siblings in their activities

- Make decisions without favoritism or prejudice
- Don't take more than their fair share
- Don't unfairly blame others
- Be fair and just in all that they do[xxiii]

Caring

Mother Theresa wrote, "Peace and war begin at home. If we truly want peace in the world, let us begin by loving one another in our own families."[xxiv] Our homes need to be homes of love and laughter, where our families experience true love and caring from each other.

Caring for and loving one another is a character trait that is also a command from God. All throughout the New Testament, we're commanded to deeply care for one another. Jesus said, *"A new command I give you: Love one another. As I have loved you, so you must love one another"* (John 13:34, NIV).

"If we truly want peace in the world, let us begin by loving one another in our own families" -Mother Theresa

One of the greatest ways to help inspire *caring* in your child is to affirm them when you see them demonstrating this character quality. You can say something like, "Hannah, I'm proud of you. I just noticed you treated your sister with kindness! Good job!" This affirmation will remind your children the importance and value of caring for each other.

Also, if you watch children's movies with your kids, when you see this character or any of the character qualities being demonstrated, ask your kids if they noticed. For example, in the movie *Cheaper by the Dozen*, Mark's brothers and sisters call him *FedEx*. Because he is so different than the rest of them, they tell Mark that the FedEx man must have delivered him. This is a great opportunity for you to say to your kids, "Now, is that very nice? Are Mark's brothers and sisters being sensitive and kind to Mark?"

We also try to give our kids opportunities to care for people. Every Christmas, our church takes a trip to a local rest home to sing songs and present gifts to the elderly. My kids have learned how good it feels to be a blessing to other people.

In Hayward, our church had a "SHOE" ministry. SHOE was an acrostic for *Sharing Hope of Eternity*. In the winter, we delivered shoes and blankets to homeless people. Our oldest daughter, Bethanie, participated in these outreaches. She saw God's love in action as she gave new shoes to many who had no shoes or worn-out shoes. She realized that she could make the world a better place by such simple acts of kindness.

Use every opportunity you can to raise children who are kind and considerate to each other and to others. Here are some ways to do so. Teach your kids to:

- Be thankful and express gratitude for what people do for them
- Forgive others for their shortcomings
- Help people in need
- Treat their siblings and friends with kindness even when they don't deserve it
- Avoid being mean, cruel, or insensitive[xxv]

The Bible says, *"Be kind and compassionate to one another, forgiving each other, just as in Christ God forgave you"* (Ephesians 4:32, NIV). This is a great verse for you and your family to memorize together as you establish the character of *caring* in their lives.

Citizenship

Citizenship is an overlooked character quality. Parents understand the importance of character traits such as honesty and respect, but we don't always realize the value of teaching good citizenship. As you establish this character trait in your children, they will learn to be more responsible about the world around them. They will learn to do their share to make their school, community, and nation a better place.[xxvi]

We need more upright children who will care about and pursue the common good, respect those in authority, and observe the laws of the land

The Bible says (Proverbs 11:11a, NLT), *"Upright citizens bless a city and make it prosper."* We need more upright children who will care about and pursue the common good, respect those in authority, and observe the laws of the land.

CHARACTER COUNTS! says that citizenship also involves being a good neighbor.[xxvii] A good neighbor helps others whenever the opportunity presents itself. The Bible says, *"Do not withhold good from those who deserve it when it's in your power to help them. If you can help your neighbor now, don't say, "Come back tomorrow, and then I'll help you"* (Proverbs 3:27-28, NLT).

Withholding *good* is inconsiderate. If your kids have an opportunity to be a blessing – to share, to fulfill a promise, or to help someone – they must learn to make the most of every opportunity to do good. Paul said, *"If you think you are too important to help someone in need, you are only fooling yourself. You are really a nobody. Be sure to do what you should"* (Galatians 6:3-4, NLT).

Here are some tips to teach your kids citizenship. Teach them to:

- Respect the property of others
- Protect the environment by recycling and not littering
- Obey laws and rules
- Play by the rules when playing games or sport activities
- Volunteer to help their church, school, or community
- Be helpful to their teachers
- Help their school and community become cleaner and safer
- Obey their parents, teachers, coaches, and others who are in an authority position[xxviii]

PRACTICAL CONSIDERATIONS

It's vital that we take the time and effort to establish character in our children. As parents, we sometimes get so caught up in getting through the day and living moment by moment that we often fail to look ahead to the type of adult we're trying to develop. If we could keep their adulthood in mind, I think we will see the value of establishing character now.

Character is not established during adulthood; it's established during the first two decades of our lives. For instance, think about someone you know who is irresponsible. An irresponsible person is someone you most likely cannot depend on. Chances are they do not show up on time, they procrastinate and often do not finish what they are supposed to finish, and they cancel on you just as easily as they commit. This character deficiency was established when they were children. They are simply demonstrating those inner qualities and traits that have been long established.

That's why we must make a conscious effort to establish our children's character now (and change our own if our character has defects). Psychologists Dr. Henry Cloud and Dr. John Townsend put it this way: "It is essential to realize that when you get Johnny to do his homework, it is not just about getting that assignment done; it is about the possible success or failure of his marriage or career."[xxix]

The character traits that your children possess have been long in the making. But don't frustrate yourself by trying to establish good character in your children in one day. "Character flaws cannot be changed overnight. Change usually takes a long period of time and involves significant relational investment and dedication."[xxx] You must stay committed to the process of character development and teach your children the right way to live.

Referring specifically to boys, Dr. James Dobson summarizes the importance of character development:

> "Parents [need] to capitalize on the impressionable years of childhood by instilling in their sons the antecedents of character. Their assignment during two brief decades will be to transform their boys from immature and flighty youngsters into honest, caring men who will be respectful of women, loyal and faithful in marriage, keepers of commitment, strong and decisive

leaders, good workers, and secure in their masculinity. And of course, the ultimate goal for people of faith is to give each child an understanding of Scripture and a lifelong passion for Jesus Christ."[xxxi]

How Will Your Kids Learn Character?

The best teacher your child will have is not at school or Sunday school. It's you. The Bible clearly shows us how kids learn. Proverbs 1:8 (NLT) says, *"Listen, my child, to what your father teaches you. Don't neglect your mother's teaching."* Similarly, Proverbs 6:20-22 (NLT) states, *"My son, obey your father's commands, and don't neglect your mother's teaching. Keep their words always in your heart. Tie them around your neck. Wherever you walk, their counsel can lead you. When you sleep, they will protect you. When you wake up in the morning, they will advise you."*

These verses tell us our kids learn from what we teach. Our words are to counsel them, lead them, protect them, advise them, guide them, and sustain them throughout their lives.

A Prayer to Pray: *Lord, I realize the value of instilling good character in my child(ren). I pray that my child(ren) will grow up demonstrating trustworthiness, respect, responsibility, fairness, caring, and citizenship. Help me to set a good example to my kids. In the areas I lack character, please help me to change these deficiencies and become more like You. And help me to instill Godly character in the life of my child(ren). Please show me how to* *raise my child(ren) so that they will become adults who make a difference in the world. In Jesus' name I pray, Amen.*

Questions to Consider:

1. What character traits do you see exhibited in your children?

2. On a scale from 1 to 5 (1 = low, 5 = high), rate your child(ren) on each of the six character traits:
    1. Trustworthiness
    2. Respect
    3. Responsibility
    4. Fairness
    5. Caring
    6. Citizenship

3. For those character traits that your kids do not score a 5 on, what can you do to help establish good character in your kids?

4. Do you need to work on any of these character traits yourself? If so, which ones.

5. If there is one thing you can immediately apply from this chapter, what would it be?

Raising Great Kids

Chapter 4

Act the Way You Want Them to Act

.

When we lived in Hayward, CA, I (Johnny) had an office in our house. I spent countless hours each week in my study reading, praying, and preparing my sermons.

When Jon-Jon was four, one day he kept coming into my office and asking if I would play with him. Each time he came, I repeated the same thing, "Jon-Jon, I'm working on my sermon. I can't play right now, but I promise, we'll play later."

I worked pretty hard that day. By late afternoon, I had finished my sermon, and I was feeling pretty relieved. I left my study in search of my little boy who had wanted to play with me all day. When I found him, he was looking at a little New Testament Bible and scribbling on a piece of paper. I asked him, "Hey, do you want to go in the backyard and play baseball with me?" In my mind I was thinking that he'd throw the Bible and his paper down, eager to play with his Daddy. Boy, was I wrong. Instead, Jon-Jon said, "I can't play right now. I'm working on my sermon."

My heart sunk!

Jon-Jon wasn't being sarcastic or vindictive. He saw that my sermon preparation was important to me, and so it became important to him. My boy wants to be just like his Dad, and it was quite obvious to me that Jon-Jon was learning from the example I had set. Unfortunately, what was taught to Jon-Jon was that my work was more important than he. I could have taken a break to play with him. In fact, a break would have probably been refreshing. I learned that if I'm going to raise my kids to live a Godly life, I must be an example worth following.

The truth is, your children will learn from the things you say, but they will learn much more from what you do. The old adage – "Do as I say, not as I do" – simply doesn't work! We must show them the way to live.

American writer James Baldwin once said, "Children have never been good at listening to their elders, but they have never failed to imitate how we treat them and others."[xxxii]

"Children have never been good at listening to their elders, but they have never failed to imitate how we treat them and others."
-James Baldwin

We often don't like the way our kids act, often because they act like us (ouch!).

Some of the Apostle Paul's strongest words are found in 1 Corinthians 11:1. He said: *"Follow my example, as I follow the example of Christ"* (NIV).

What a statement! Paul challenged the people of Corinth to literally "mimic" his actions and attitudes because he was living a Christ-like life.

What if we were able to say these words to our children? Kids, follow my example, because I am following the example of Christ. I am loving others unconditionally like Christ. I am forgiving graciously like Christ. I am giving sacrificially like Christ. In humility, I am considering others better than myself, like Christ.

What if our children were able to see our Christ-likeness demonstrated in our daily lives? What if they saw our devotion to Bible reading, prayer, and even handling difficulties in a Christ-like way? If we truly lived in a Christ-like way, it would make all the difference. Our children would imitate us as we imitate Christ, and the result would be children who act the way we want them to.

Being a Model to Follow

The famous church leaders John and Charles Wesley both attribute their commitment to God to the example set by their mother, Susannah. Even though there were 17 children in the family, their Mom was dedicated to having a time where she would read the Bible and pray. It was quite challenging, since the house was small and there were so many children. Yet she managed to spend time alone with God. She would go into the kitchen, sit on a stool, and put an apron over her head as she read God's Word and prayed. The kids knew not to disturb her during this time. As soon as the apron came off, then they could talk to their Mom again.

Susannah Wesley, mother of 17 children, was dedicated to having a time where she would read and pray

This dedication to prayer and God's Word left a lasting impression on the Wesley children. They knew that spending time with God was important because they saw it lived out right in front of them. Susannah didn't have to say, "Children, reading God's Word is important." The children saw how important it was to their Mom.

It's like the story of the four Bible scholars who were arguing over the best Bible translation. One said he preferred the King James Version because of its beauty and eloquent old English. Another said he liked the New American Standard Version for its literalism and how it moved the reader from passage to passage with confident feelings of accuracy from the original text. The third scholar was sold on the New Living Translation for its use of contemporary phrases and idioms that captured the meaning of difficult ideas.

After being quiet for a moment, the fourth scholar admitted: "I have personally preferred my mother's translation." The other scholars started laughing, and one of them said, "Your Mom didn't translate the Bible." The fourth scholar said, "Yes, she did. My mom translated the Bible into life, and it was the most convincing translation I ever saw."

We want to ask you a very challenging question. It's a question we ask ourselves, also. What kind of Bible does your child read when he or she observes your life?

It's not too late to be a Godly example to your children. You can make that commitment today, to strive to live like Christ in

> *What kind of Bible does your child read when he or she observes your life?*

all you do. It begins with a simple prayer, *"Lord Jesus, I want to be like you. Please make me more like you."* The Bible says that God knows your heart, and as you commit to living in a Christ-like way, He will give you the strength and power to set a Godly example for your children so that you can say with all confidence, "Follow my example, as I follow the example of Christ."

We're Held Accountable

There are several passages of Scripture that emphasize how important it is for us to make sure children are not led astray. There is no doubt that Jesus loves children. He loves them so much that He is holding us accountable to raise them right. Jesus said, *"If anyone causes one of these little ones who believe in me to sin,* it would be better for him to have a large millstone hung around his neck and to be drowned in the depths of the sea" (Matthew 18:6, NIV).

We don't know about you, but this verse motivates us to do all we can to live rightly in front of our children. If they pick up ungodly attitudes and prejudices from our lives, then we are causing them to sin. If they hear us tell white lies to get out of appointments or meetings, they're learning from us that they can be dishonest also.

God holds parents and other adults who influence children accountable for how they shape these young lives. We must be a consistently good example for our kids to follow. There's not too much that goes unnoticed in the eyes of our children. Let them notice you living like Christ in all you do.

PRACTICAL CONSIDERATIONS

Be aware of your behavior. If your kids are modeling behavior you don't like, make sure they haven't learned it from you. Even though a popular survey showed that only 39% of teenagers want to be like their parents,[xxxiii] the fact is that all teenagers are like their parents in some way. They learn from the example set by their parents.

A Prayer to Pray: *"Heavenly Father, because my children are going to be just like me, help me to be just like You. I have a lot of growing to do; please don't let me get discouraged as I learn how* *to be more Christ-like in all I do and say. I ask You to reveal to me anything in my life that needs to change. Make me like You, I pray in Jesus' name, Amen."*

Questions to Consider:

1. Am I the most Godly man or woman my child has ever met?

2. Is my life worth mimicking?

3. Is there anything in my life right now that needs to change? What steps do I need to take to make that change?

Chapter 5

Teach Them to Dream about Their Future

Raising Great Kids

God is a God who is interested in our future. He has a plan for every man, woman, and child. He clearly tells us in Jeremiah 29:11 (NIV), "'I know the plans I have for you,' declares the LORD, 'plans to prosper you and not to harm you, plans to give you hope and a future.'"

If God wants to give our children a hope and a future, we must help our children discover God's plan for their lives. If you help your kids discover and fulfill their God-given dreams, the Bible promises them true fulfillment. Proverbs 13:12 (NLT) says, *"Hope deferred makes the heart sick, but when dreams come true, there is life and joy."* We want to encourage you to intentionally help your children experience life and joy.

> *Every parent has the potential of becoming a dreambuilder or a dreambuster*

Every parent has the potential of becoming a dreambuilder or a dreambuster. Parents are great at becoming dreambuilders when their children are young.

It's fun to ask children what they want to do when they grow up. Our five-year old Daniel, and our seven-year-old Jon-Jon, want to be professional baseball players who play on the San Francisco Giants. Our nine-year-old, Hannah, wants to be a professional gymnast or a ballerina. Our ten-year old Bethanie wants to become an actress and/or a professional musician. They each have aspirations and dreams.

Of course, just like you, we will try to build confidence in our kids and tell them, "The sky is the limit, honey, you can become anything you want to become." And when they tell us things like, "I want to be a professional ballerina," we think it's charming.

The older your child gets, however, his or her ambitions might become less and less charming. When your child is fifteen and she still wants to become a ballerina, our response might be: "But how are you going to make a living doing that!" Or in the case of our ten-year old, we're tempted to stifle her dream about becoming a professional musician since we know how difficult it is – nearly impossible – to break into the music industry. And that's when we can unfortunately shift from being a dreambuilder to a dreambuster.

With our daughter, Bethanie, we have helped show her that her dream of singing can be used for God. When Bethanie says she wants to be a professional singer, we know she has Hilary Duff and fame and fortune on her mind. But we're teaching her that her musical gifts and talents can be used for God to have an even greater impact. I (Johnny) recently told Bethanie, "You might not ever make a CD that's distributed around the world on a major label, but perhaps God will use a CD you produce to make a difference in the lives of many others." I told her that fame and fortune will not make her happy. What will truly make her happy is using her time and gifts to serve and bless other people. This was exciting to Bethanie, because ultimately, she wants to make a difference with her life.

"He who pursues worthless things lacks sense" -Proverbs 12:11b, NAS

64

So many people give their lives to useless things. The Bible says, *"He who pursues worthless things lacks sense"* (Proverbs 12:11b, NAS). The Good News Translation (GNT) states this verse a little more bluntly: *"It is stupid to waste time on useless projects."*

We must teach our kids to make a contribution with their lives. Here's how to get started:

PRACTICAL CONSIDERATIONS
Seek God's Direction

"What is God's dream for my child's life?"

As I mentioned at the beginning of this chapter, Jeremiah 29:11 says that God has a plan for everyone's life. The question we must ask is, "What is God's dream for my child's life?" If they pursue a dream that does not line up with His plan for their lives, God will not bless that dream. The Bible says, *"We can make our plans, but the LORD determines our steps"* (Proverbs 16:9, NLT). Similarly, Proverbs 19:21 (NLT) says, *"You can make many plans, but the LORD'S purpose will prevail."*

Because God's purposes and plans for your child will prevail, seek God's direction for their lives. Pray with your children about their aspirations and dreams. During your quiet time with the Lord, ask God to speak to your child about his or her God-given dreams.

Ask God for his guidance and direction for their lives. With God's power and strength, he will help your children (and you, too) fulfill their dreams. The Bible says, *"Now glory be to God, who by his mighty power at work within us is able to do far more than we would ever dare to ask or even dream of - infinitely beyond our highest prayers, desires, thoughts, or hopes"* (Ephesians 3:20, TLB).

Help Them Explore

No dream your child can dream is too big. Help them explore big dreams.

In a book titled *Dream Makers: Young People Share Their Hopes and Aspirations,* Neil Waldman reveals the dreams that are in the hearts and minds of children across America. Written in either rhymes or free verse, many of the dreams are the typical American dreams, such as owning mansions or having tons of money. Some of the dreams are charming, like having a lifetime supply of chocolate. But some of the dreams are heartfelt expressions of children's hopes and ambitions, such as finding a cure for cancer, saving the environment, and achieving peace. One fifth grader shared the following dream: "There is peace in the Middle East/and threats of terrorism/are gone/I am not afraid to/let my children/go outside."[xxxiv]

To help your kids explore their dreams, ask them, "If you could make a difference in the world, what would you do?" You can also help them explore how it may benefit others. For example, ask them, "Could others benefit if your dream is fulfilled?"

If your kids do not have any ideas of what their dreams may be, there are some steps you can take to help them explore their future. In *Dreambuilders,* Kathy Peel recommends taking your kids through the following exercise:

- Write down three things you have enjoyed doing and would like to do some more.

- Write down three things you would like to try.
- Write down three hobbies that sound fun.
- Write down three skills you would like to learn.[xxxv]

Such questions will get your kids thinking about things that might help reveal their future dreams.

Emphasize Your Child's Uniqueness

In Chapter 2, we talked about how we should train our children based on their uniqueness and their natural bent. We must do the same when it comes to their dreams. Peel says, "As parents, we need to be dreambuilders, considering our kids' unique makeup and budding dreams. When we communicate that God uniquely gifted them for a special purpose and we want to help them discover and pursue it, this is perhaps the greatest gift we can give our children."[xxxvi]

Our temptation has been to try to inspire our children with our dreams. But our four children are completely different from each other, and their dreams will be completely different than ours. And we're learning to encourage them to dream big dreams based on their own uniqueness.

Affirm them

Even if your child's dream doesn't seem realistic or of interest to you, encourage your child. This affirmation will not only build your child's self-esteem, it will help them share their plans with you and not be embarrassed to dream with you. Kathy Peel concludes, "Either we will wisely guide and cheer them on their way, or we will deflate their aspirations."[xxxvii]

Teach your children to dream big dreams. At the same time, we want to encourage you to dream new dreams. One of those dreams can be to raise your children to live right, walk tall, and demonstrate the type of character that will sustain them for the rest of their lives.

In the movie *Cheaper by the Dozen,* Tom Baker (played by Steve Martin) accepts his dream job of being head coach at a major university. He resigns at the end of the season because the job robs him of spending time with his family. In a meeting with Shake, the director of athletics, the following conversation takes place:

> Baker says, "I'm resigning after this season, Shake."
> "Giving up the dream?" Shake asks.
> "No, I'm just going with a different one," Baker replies.
> Shake asks, "No regrets?"
> Then Baker says something profound: "If I screw up raising my kids, nothing I achieve will matter much."

I hope these words will resonate within you as you seek to raise great kids!

A Prayer to Pray: *"Dear Heavenly Father, please help me to be a dreambuilder and a dream releaser. Help me to encourage my child(ren) to dream God-sized dreams. As I help my child(ren) discover their dreams, please inspire me to dream big dreams and to think about how I can make a difference in the world. Thank you for giving me and my child(ren) a hope and a future, in Jesus' name I pray, Amen.*

Questions to Consider:

1. What did you dream about becoming when you were a child?

2. Have you put *your* dreams aside, or are you still dreaming big dreams?

3. What is one thing you can immediately do to help your child(ren) begin to dream?

Resource A

Key Scripture Passages Relating to Parenting

Scriptures Regarding Parents' Responsibilities

"Fathers, do not exasperate your children; instead, bring them up in the training and instruction of the Lord." Ephesians 6:4 (NIV)

"Fathers, do not embitter your children, or they will become discouraged." Colossians 3:21 (NIV)

"The righteous man leads a blameless life; blessed are his children after him." Proverbs 20:7 (NIV)

"A wife of noble character who can find? She is worth far more than rubies…Her children arise and call her blessed; her husband also, and he praises her." Proverbs 31:10;27 (NIV)

"I was young and now I am old, yet I have never seen the righteous forsaken or their children begging bread. They are always generous and lend freely; their children will be blessed." Psalm 37:25-26 (NIV)

"Only be careful, and watch yourselves closely so that you do not forget the things your eyes have seen or let them slip from your heart as long as you live. Teach them to your children and to their children after them." Deuteronomy 4:9 (NIV)

"Love the LORD your God with all your heart and with all your soul and with all your strength. These commandments that I give you today are to be upon your hearts. Impress them on your children. Talk about them when you sit at home and when you walk along the road, when you lie down and when you get up. Tie them as symbols on your hands and bind them on your foreheads. Write them on the doorframes of your houses and on your gates." Deuteronomy 6:5-9 (NIV)

"Fix these words of mine in your hearts and minds; tie them as symbols on your hands and bind them on your foreheads. Teach them to your children, talking about them when you sit at home and when you walk along the road, when you lie down and when you get up. Write them on the doorframes of your houses and on your gates, so that your days and the days of your children may be many in the land that the LORD swore to give your forefathers, as many as the days that the heavens are above the earth." Deuteronomy 11:18-21 (NIV)

"Train a child in the way he should go, and when he is old he will not turn from it." Proverbs 22:6 (NIV)

"For I, too, was once my father's son, tenderly loved by my mother as an only child. My father told me, "Take my words to heart. Follow my instructions and you will live. Learn to be wise, and develop good judgment. Don't forget or turn away from my words." Proverbs 4:3-5 (NLT)

"We will not hide these truths [stories of God's faithfulness] *from our children but will tell the next generation about the glorious deeds of the LORD. We will tell of his power and the mighty miracles he did."* Psalm 78:1-4 (NLT)

Resource A

Scriptures Regarding Children's Responsibilities

"Listen, my child, to what your father teaches you. Don't neglect your mother's teaching. What you learn from them will crown you with grace and clothe you with honor." Proverbs 1:8-9 (NLT)

"Listen, my son, and be wise, and keep your heart on the right path." Proverbs 23:19 (NIV)

"Listen to your father, who gave you life, and do not despise your mother when she is old." Proverbs 23:22 (NIV)

"My son, obey your father's commands, and don't neglect your mother's teaching. Keep their words always in your heart. Tie them around your neck. Wherever you walk, their counsel can lead you. When you sleep, they will protect you. When you wake up in the morning, they will advise you. For these commands and this teaching are a lamp to light the way ahead of you. The correction of discipline is the way to life." Proverbs 6:20-23 (NLT)

"Children, obey your parents in the Lord, for this is right. 'Honor your father and mother' - which is the first commandment with a promise – 'that it may go well with you and that you may enjoy long life on the earth.'" Ephesians 6:1-3 (NIV)

"Children, obey your parents in everything, for this pleases the Lord." Colossians 3:20 (NIV)

"A wise child accepts a parent's discipline; a young mocker refuses to listen." Proverbs 13:1 (NLT)

"Only a fool despises a parent's discipline; whoever learns from correction is wise." Proverbs 15:5 (NLT)

"A wise son brings joy to his father, but a foolish son grief to his mother." Proverbs 10:1 (NIV)

Resource B

Internet Resources to Help You Raise Great Kids

There are many great books in print that are helpful in raising great kids. We have also found many websites to be helpful, including those listed below. Please be aware that Internet content changes frequently. At the time of this writing, these sites provided helpful tips and encouragement for parents.

1. www.allprodad.com
2. www.familyfirst.net
3. www.family.org
4. www.cpyu.org
5. www.christianitytoday.com/parenting
6. www.mops.org
7. www.crosswalk.com/family/parenting
8. www.charactercounts.org
9. www.charactercrew.com

Resource C

Devotion Ideas for Great Family Devotions

For basic family devotions, all you really need is a dedicated time slot that you spend with your family. Sometimes you may want to read a Bible verse or Bible story; other times you may just want to talk with your kids about their day and then pray with them. No matter what you do, always end with a time of prayer. Give your kids an opportunity to express things they would like to pray about. Sometimes you may have each member of the family pray. Other times you might be the only one who prays.

These family devotions will help draw your family closer together and create lasting memories. We encourage you to schedule this time. Prioritize it! Protect it!

You can keep your time of devotions fairly basic (Bible reading and/or prayer), or you may want to be more creative. If you choose the creative option, here are some ideas to help you get started.

1. Dramatize the Parables. In Matthew, Luke, and John, there are many different parables that Jesus used to illustrate lessons he was teaching. You can dramatize these parables, having your kids act out the parts as you read.[xxxviii] Here are some parables from Matthew, for example, that would work well:

- Parable of the Lost Sheep – Matthew 18:10-14
- Parable of the Unmerciful Servant – Matthew 18:21-35
- Parable of the Workers in the Vineyard - Matthew 20:1-16 (you be the landowner)
- Parable of the Talents - Matthew 25:14-30

2. Finish the Sentence, "God is..." This is a great way to get your family thinking about how awesome God is. Ask each family member to come up with as many possible ways they can to finish the sentence, "God is. . ." If they are able to write, you can even have each person write down his or her responses on a piece of paper. Then you can post this list of the attributes of God in a prominent location in your house.[xxxix]

3. Use Metaphors. When you gather with your family for a time of devotions, ask each child to look around the room and find objects that represent a character or quality of God. For example, "God is like this chair, because I can fully put my trust in Him, knowing He will be able to support me no matter what I am going through."[xl] If you can think of any Scripture verses that coincide with the metaphor, make sure to bring it up. Keep going from person to person until you run out of objects to talk about.

4. Express Thanks. Sometimes we only express thanks at Thanksgiving time. But God wants us to continually have grateful hearts for all He has done. Read a Bible verse that emphasizes thanksgiving. For example, Psalm 105:1 (NIV) says, *"Give thanks to the LORD, call on his name; make known among the*

78

nations what he has done." Then have each family member write down (you may need to write it down for a child who can't write yet) on a piece of paper 5 to 10 things they are thankful for and then share those reasons with each other.[xli] We'd advise you to collect those pieces of paper and save them as things to treasure.

5. Devise a Family Prayer Calendar. Using an ordinary calendar, fill in each day for this month with things for your family to pray about. You can write in the names of people, events, issues, or decisions, just to name a few prayer ideas. At your time of family devotions, use your prayer calendar to help you focus your prayers. In addition, if the family prayer calendar is hung in a prominent location, you can also remember to pray about the things listed on the calendar at meal times and throughout the day. Just make sure you try to pray regularly. "Praying regularly will keep you accountable for praying for what is written on the calendar and will also help you form a habit of praying together as a family."[xlii]

There are endless ideas of things you can do during your family devotions. The key is to spend time with your family as you nurture their spiritual well being.

Raising Great Kids

Resource D

Scripture Verses for Your Family to Memorize

Scripture memorization is our foundation for right living. The Psalmist said, *"I have hidden your word in my heart that I might not sin against you"* (Psalm 119:11, NIV).

Joshua said, *"Do not let this Book of the Law depart from your mouth; meditate on it day and night, so that you may be careful to do everything written in it. Then you will be prosperous and successful"* (Joshua 1:8, NIV). Here are several key Bible verses to assist you in your journey of helping your children to love God and hate wrong doing.

Character Building Bible Verses
"Be kind and compassionate to one another, forgiving each other, just as in Christ God forgave you." Ephesians 4:32 (NIV)

"Make sure that nobody pays back wrong for wrong, but always try to be kind to each other and to everyone else." 1 Thessalonians 5:15 (NIV)

"Each of you should look not only to your own interests, but also to the interests of others." Philippians 2:4 (NIV)

"Do to others as you would have them do to you." Luke 6:31 (NIV)

"But I tell you who hear me: Love your enemies, do good to those who hate you, bless those who curse you, pray for those who mistreat you." Luke 6:27-28 (NIV)

"Don't repay evil for evil. Don't retaliate when people say unkind things about you. Instead, pay them back with a blessing. That is what God wants you to do, and he will bless you for it." 1 Peter 3:9 (NLT)

"Do not forget to do good and to share with others, for with such sacrifices God is pleased." Hebrews 13:16 (NIV)

"Whatever you do, work at it with all your heart, as working for the Lord, not for men, since you know that you will receive an inheritance from the Lord as a reward." Colossians 3:23-24 (NIV)

"Don't let anyone look down on you because you are young, but set an example for the believers in speech, in life, in love, in faith and in purity." 1 Timothy 4:12 (NIV)

"I praise you because I am fearfully and wonderfully made; your works are wonderful, I know that full well." Psalm 139:14 (NIV)

"God saw all that he had made, and it was very good." Genesis 1:31 (NIV)

"The LORD does not look at the things man looks at. Man looks at the outward appearance, but the LORD looks at the heart." 1 Samuel 16:7b (NIV)

Godly Living

"Be joyful always; pray continually; give thanks in all circumstances, for this is God's will for you in Christ Jesus." 1 Thessalonians 5:16-17 (NIV)

"Trust in the LORD with all your heart and lean not on your own understanding; in all your ways acknowledge him, and he will make your paths straight." Proverbs 3:5-6 (NIV)

"Listen, my son, and be wise, and keep your heart on the right path." Proverbs 23:19 (NIV)

"Whatever is true, whatever is noble, whatever is right, whatever is pure, whatever is lovely, whatever is admirable - if anything is excellent or praiseworthy - think about such things." Philippians 4:8 (NIV)

"For the eyes of the LORD range throughout the earth to strengthen those whose hearts are fully committed to him." 2 Chronicles 16:9 (NIV)

"Don't worry about anything; instead, pray about everything. Tell God what you need, and thank him for all he has done. If you do this, you will experience God's peace, which is far more wonderful than the human mind can understand. His peace will guard your hearts and minds as you live in Christ Jesus." Philippians 4:6-7 (NLT)

"You will seek me and find me when you seek me with all your heart." Jeremiah 29:13 (NIV)

"Set your minds on things above, not on earthly things." Colossians 3:2 (NIV)

"So be careful how you live, not as fools but as those who are wise. Make the most of every opportunity for doing good in these evil." Ephesians 5:15-16 (NLT)

Promises of God's Help
"I can do everything through him who gives me strength." Philippians 4:13 (NIV)

"Ah, Sovereign LORD, you have made the heavens and the earth by your great power and outstretched arm. Nothing is too hard for you." Jeremiah 32:17 (NIV)

"I am the LORD, the God of all mankind. Is anything too hard for me?" Jeremiah 32:27 (NIV)

A Scripture about God's Plan for Our Lives
"For I know the plans I have for you," declares the LORD, "plans to prosper you and not to harm you, plans to give you hope and a future." Jeremiah 29:11 (NIV)

Promises of God's Protection and Guidance
"I will guide you along the best pathway for your life. I will advise you and watch over you." Psalm 32:8 (NLT)

"The LORD will keep you from all harm - he will watch over your life." Psalm 121:7 (NIV)

"But those who hope in the LORD will renew their strength. They will soar on wings like eagles; they will run and not grow weary, they will walk and not be faint." Isaiah 40:31 (NIV)

"The LORD will guide you always; he will satisfy your needs in a sunscorched land and will strengthen your frame. You will be like a well-watered garden, like a spring whose waters never fail." Isaiah 58:11 (NIV)

Salvation Scriptures

"For all have sinned and fall short of the glory of God." Romans 3:23 (NIV)

"Everyone who calls on the name of the Lord will be saved." Romans 10:13 (NIV)

"If you confess with your mouth, 'Jesus is Lord,' and believe in your heart that God raised him from the dead, you will be saved. For it is with your heart that you believe and are justified, and it is with your mouth that you confess and are saved." Romans 10:9-10 (NIV)

"If we confess our sins, he is faithful and just and will forgive us our sins and purify us from all unrighteousness." 1 John 1:9 (NIV)

"For God so loved the world that he gave his one and only Son, that whoever believes in him shall not perish but have eternal life." John 3:16 (NIV)

The Importance of God's Word

"Do not let this Book of the Law depart from your mouth; meditate on it day and night, so that you may be careful to do everything written in it. Then you will be prosperous and successful." Joshua 1:8 (NIV)

"How can a young man keep his way pure? By living according to your word." Psalm 119:9 (NIV)

"I have hidden your word in my heart that I might not sin against you." Psalm 119:11 (NIV)

"Your word is a lamp to my feet and a light for my path." Psalm 119:105 (NIV)

Excellent Passages of Scripture to Memorize

The following Scripture passages are longer and can be memorized over a series of weeks/months. Have each family member memorize one verse a week until the entire passage is memorized. You may even want to consider a reward for everyone when the Scripture is memorized.

1 Corinthians 13:4-13
Galatians 5:22-26
Psalm 23
Psalm 100
Matthew 11:28-30
Matthew 22:37-40
Luke 11:2-4
John 15:12-15
1 Peter 3:10-13

Afterword

This book is a tool to help you raise kids with the help of Christ Jesus. However, if you've never established a personal relationship with Jesus, the first step you need to take is to invite Him into your life to be your Lord and Savior. God wants to give you a brand new start for your life. You can begin your journey with Jesus and invite Him into your life by praying this simple prayer.

> *Jesus Christ, thank you for giving me the Word of God that shows me the right way to live. Please come into my heart and life. I don't want to live for myself anymore; I want to live for you. I want to experience the joy and peace that only you can bring to me. Please forgive me of all the wrong things I've done. Please come into my heart and be my Lord and Savior, the One who is in control of my life. As best as I know how, I give my life to you! In Your name I pray, Amen.*

If you said this prayer and sincerely meant it, the Bible promises you that you are saved and have been given a new life. We encourage you to commit yourself to regular church attendance where you can begin to grow in your new relationship with Jesus. If you live in the Tucson area, we warmly welcome you to check out Pathway of Hope Foursquare

Church. Visit us on the web at www.pathwayofhope.net. Please feel free to email us at pastorjohnnyj@pathwayofhope.net to learn more about the next steps to take as a new believer in Christ Jesus.

May God bless you and give you wisdom and guidance as you raise your children to be great kids in a not-so-great world.

Johnny & Melynda Johnson

About the Authors

Jonathan and Melynda are the pastors of Pathway of Hope Foursquare Church in Tucson, AZ. The couple served as pastors of New Hope Christian Fellowship, Hayward, CA, from 2000 to 2005. They served as ministers of music at Faith Center Church in Eureka, CA, from 1992 to 2000. Both Jonathan and Melynda are licensed and ordained pastors through the Foursquare Church. Jonathan is currently an adjunct professor at Patten University in Oakland, CA, and LIFE Pacific College in San Dimas, CA.

Melynda earned a Bachelor of Practical Ministry from the Wagner Leadership Institute in Colorado Springs, CO. Jonathan holds a B.A. from the University of California, Davis, an M.A. in Christian Ministry from Simpson University, Redding, CA, a Doctor of Practical Ministry from the Wagner Leadership Institute in Colorado Springs, CO, and is currently a PhD candidate at Capella University, Minneapolis, MN. Jonathan and Melynda have four GREAT children: Bethanie, Hannah, Jon-Jon, and Daniel. They reside in Oro Valley, Arizona.

Notes

Chapter 1

[i] Charlene C. Giannetti & Margaret Sagarese, *The Roller-Coaster Years* (New York: Broadway Books, 1997), p. 127.

[ii] Interview with Dr. Phil Interview on NBC News' MEET THE PRESS, Sunday, December 26, 2004.

[iii] Rick Warren, *The Purpose Driven Life* (Grand Rapids, MI: Zondervan, 2002), p. 127.

[iv] Warren, p. 125.

[v] Warren, p. 127.

[vi] Greg Smalley, "Turning Your Natural Parenting Style into a Blessing." Retrieved August 2005 from http://www.crosswalk.com/family/parenting/kids/794834.html?view=print.

[vii] Warren, p. 128.

[viii] Peter Scales & Nancy Leffert, *Developmental Assets* (Minneapolis, MN: Search Institute, 1999), p. 24.

[ix] Scales & Leffert, pp. 24-25.

[x] Erma Bombeck, *The Green, Green Grass of Home* (November 1971). Retrieved August 2005 from http://www.new-life.net/favrt013.htm.

[xi] "A Hundred Years From Now." Retrieved August 2005 from http://www.venturatoday.net/100years.html.

[xii] Mother Theresa, *In My Own Words* (New York: Gramercy Books, 1996), p. 51.

[xiii] "Laughter May be Good for the Heart," Reuter's News, March 9, 2005.

[xiv] John Trent, "Strength Training," *Christian Parenting Today*, July/August 1995.

[xv] Lindsey O'Connor, *If Mama Ain't Happy, Ain't Nobody Happy!* (Eugene, OR: Harvest House, 1996), p. 231.

[xvi] Warren, p. 127.

Chapter 3

[xvii] See www.charactercounts.org.

[xviii] Traci Pedone, "The Essentials of a Healthy Home." Retrieved August 2005 from http://www.focusonyourchild.com/faith/art1/A0000526.html.

[xix] See www.charactercounts.org.

[xx] "Respect," *Focus on the Family's Focus on Your Child*. Retrieved August 2005 from http://www.focusonyourchild.com/develop/charactercrew/respect.html.

[xxi] See www.charactercounts.org and www.charactercrew.com

[xxii] *Ibid.*

[xxiii] *Ibid.*

[xxiv] Theresa, p. 47.

[xxv] See www.charactercounts.org.

[xxvi] See www.charactercrew.com.

[xxvii] See www. charactercounts.org.

[xxviii] See www.charactercrew.com and charactercounts.org.

[xxix] Henry Cloud & John Townsend, *Boundaries With Kids* (Grand Rapids, MI: Zondervan, 1998), p. 23.

[xxx] John Maxwell, *Developing the Leaders Around You* (Thomas Nelson, 1995), p. 48.

[xxxi] James Dobson, "Our Ultimate Priority as Parents." Retrieved August 2005 from http://www.focusonyourchild.com/develop/art1/A0000704.html.

Chapter 4

[xxxii] "Respect," *Focus on the Family's Focus on Your Child.* Retrieved August 2005 from http://www.focusonyourchild.com/develop/charactercrew/respect.html.

[xxxiii] Charis Conn & Ilena Silverman, *What Counts: The Complete Harper's Index* (New York: Holt, 1991).

Chapter 5

[xxxiv] Neil Waldman, *Dream Makers: Young People Share Their Hopes and Aspirations* (Honesdale, PA: Boyds Mill Press, 2003).

[xxxv] Kathy Peel, "Dreambuilders," *Focus on the Family Magazine* (February 2005), p. 23

[xxxvi] *Ibid.*

[xxxvii] *Ibid.*

Resource D

[xxxviii] This idea was adapted from "Calling Godly Parents," retrieved August 2005 from http://www.focusonyourchild.com/faith/art1/A0000482.html.

[xxxix] *52 Family Devotional Ideas.* Retrieved August 2005 from http://www.srtmrocks.org/pages/parent%27s%20page?multcontentitemid=175234.

[xl] *Ibid.*

[xli] *Ibid.*

[xlii] *Ibid.*